Swish Swoosh

Kelly Doudna

Consulting Editor, Monica Marx, M.A./Reading Specialist

Published by SandCastle™, an imprint of ABDO Publishing Company, 4940 Viking Drive, Edina, Minnesota 55435.

Printed in the United States.

Credits
Edited by: Pam Price
Curriculum Coordinator: Nancy Tuminelly
Cover and Interior Design and Production: Mighty Media
Photo Credits: Brand X Pictures, Comstock, Corbis Images, Hemera, Image 100, PhotoDisc, Rubberball Productions

Library of Congress Cataloging-in-Publication Data

Doudna, Kelly, 1963-
     Swish swoosh / Kelly Doudna.
       p. cm. -- (Sound words)
     Includes index.
     Summary: Uses photographs and simple sentences to introduce words that sound like what they mean: sizzle, crackle, glug, slurp, swoosh, fizz, shatter, crinkle, tinkle, fizzle.
     ISBN 1-59197-454-2
     1. English language--Onomatopoeic words--Juvenile literature. 2. Sounds, Words for--Juvenile literature. [1. English language--Onomatopoeic words. 2. Sounds, Words for.] I. Title.

PE1597.D65 2003
428.1--dc21

2003044338

SandCastle™ books are created by a professional team of educators, reading specialists, and content developers around five essential components that include phonemic awareness, phonics, vocabulary, text comprehension, and fluency. All books are written, reviewed, and leveled for guided reading, early intervention reading, and Accelerated Reader® programs and designed for use in shared, guided, and independent reading and writing activities to support a balanced approach to literacy instruction.

Let Us Know

After reading the book, SandCastle would like you to tell us your stories about reading. What is your favorite page? Was there something hard that you needed help with? Share the ups and downs of learning to read. We want to hear from you! To get posted on the ABDO Publishing Company Web site, send us e-mail at:

sandcastle@abdopub.com

SandCastle Level: Transitional

Onomatopoeia (on-uh-mat-uh-**pee**-uh) is the use of words that sound like what they describe.

These **sound words** are all around us.

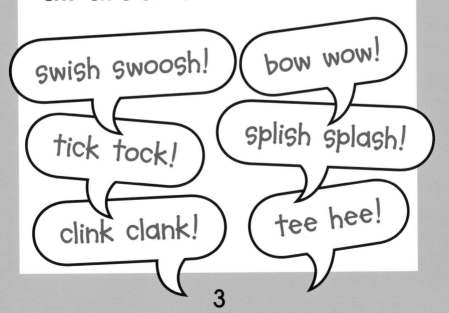

Mary's grandpa grills burgers.

Sizzle!

Will and his dad sit by
the fire.

Crackle!

Deb drinks milk.

Glug!

Lucy licks an
ice-cream cone.

Slurp!

Theo throws a
basketball.

Swish!

Paul has soda pop
with his snack.

Fizz!

The window breaks with a shatter.

Forks and spoons rattle with a clatter.

Paper crumples with a crinkle.

Wind chimes ting with a tinkle.

Bacon fries with a sizzle.

20

Soda pop bubbles with a fizzle.

Picture Index

clatter, p. 17

crackle, p. 7

fizz, p. 15

sizzle, pp. 5, 20

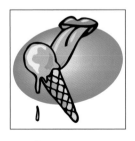

slurp, p. 11

swish, p. 13

Glossary

crumple   to crush something, such a piece of paper, out of shape

grill   to cook food on a grill

rattle   to make a quick series of sharp short sounds

snack   a little bit of food eaten between meals

wind chimes   a group of small bells or metal tubes hung together that move in the wind, making a musical sound

About SandCastle™

A professional team of educators, reading specialists, and content developers created the SandCastle™ series to support young readers as they develop reading skills and strategies and increase their general knowledge. The SandCastle™ series has four levels that correspond to early literacy development in young children. The levels are provided to help teachers and parents select the appropriate books for young readers.

Emerging Readers
(no flags)

Beginning Readers
(1 flag)

Transitional Readers
(2 flags)

Fluent Readers
(3 flags)

These levels are meant only as a guide. All levels are subject to change.

To see a complete list of SandCastle™ books and other nonfiction titles from ABDO Publishing Company, visit www.abdopub.com or contact us at:

4940 Viking Drive, Edina, Minnesota 55435 • 1-800-800-1312 • fax: 1-952-831-1632